Fighting Fires
Then and Now

by Ann Rossi
illustrated by Steve Snider

 HOUGHTON MIFFLIN　　　BOSTON

People have been fighting fires for thousands of years. But they haven't always had fire engines to help put out fires!

Hundreds of years ago in America, people used buckets filled with water to put out fires. They needed lots of water, and they needed it quickly.

Sometimes the water was far away from the fire. That's why people formed two lines called *bucket brigades*. A bucket of water was handed down the line until it reached the person closest to the fire. He or she threw the water on the flames.

Then the empty bucket was passed along the second line. Finally, the bucket got back to the water, where it was filled again.

4

It took a long time to pass buckets of water. Sometimes bucket brigades couldn't put out fires. Many houses were made of wood. Houses were also built very close together. Fires spread quickly from one house to the next.

People knew that they had to do something about the fires. They started using fire pumps with tanks. Firefighters filled the tanks with water. Then they pulled the fire pumps to the fire. Next, they had to pump the water out by hand. Many firefighters were needed to pump the water.

The water from these fire pumps shot through a short hose onto the fire. Now firefighters didn't need to stand next to a fire to put it out. But they had to keep filling the tank with water. Otherwise it would soon be empty.

More than one hundred fifty years ago, a fire pump that ran on steam was invented. It didn't take as many people to work this fire pump. It was pulled by horses and could get to a fire more quickly than hand-pulled fire pumps. It could also spray water onto a fire from farther away. This made it safer for the firefighters.

About one hundred years ago, gas engines replaced steam engines. Fire engines that ran on gas did not need to be pulled by horses. They could be driven like cars.

Some fire engines that ran on gas carried ladders.

Others had long hoses.

As the years went by, fire engines carried more and more kinds of gear. Today's fire engines and firefighters are ready for all kinds of emergencies!